MW01244809

MISPLACED

DISCOVER YOUR PURPOSE IN THE PROPHETIC PLAN OF GOD

ISAAC WATSON

TABLE OF CONTENTS

ENDORSEMENTS

I recommend this new addition on the subject of the prophetic by Isaac Watson. This book will bring clarity and understanding concerning the different functions of prophetic people. It will help you identify your calling so that you can walk in it effectively. The Lord is giving us more clarity and understanding concerning the prophetic ministry and intercession. I encourage you to explore the truths in this book and continue to grow in your knowledge of the prophetic realm.

John Eckhardt
Best-selling Author of Prayers That Rout Demons

Isaac Watson is an insightful communicator who masterfully articulates the prophetic mindset and function in this book. There is a longing for authentic prophets and prophetic ministry in the earth, and this teaching equips people to rise and meet the moment.

Ryan LeStrange
Author of Breaking Curses and many other titles

I wish I'd read this book 30 years ago! With prophetic precision my friend Isaac Watson brings clarity to believers who are asking, "What's my function: Intercessor or Prophet?" For anyone looking to grow in their spiritual gifts and intimacy with the Lord, this book is a must read. Finding peace in your calling and function in the body of Christ is vital for spiritual maturity. In this urgent hour, you must come out of any confusion and into your calling. Read "Misplaced" today and find your place in God's kingdom.

Will Ford, Co-Founder of 818 The Sign
Author of "The Dream King: How the Dream of Martin Luther King Jr. Is Being Fulfilled to Heal Racism In America."
Dreamsteamco.com
818thesign.org

FOREWORD

I am excited and honored that I get to write the foreword to this new book *Misplaced*. I have known Isaac Watson for over 15 years. God has given me the honor and great joy to be his spiritual mother. I met him in a youth meeting where I was activating him and many others in the art of hearing the voice of God. Isaac stood out to me as a passionate teenager who loved the word of God and prayed with great fervency. I am delighted to say the same is true today. Isaac has developed into a wise master builder to the body of Christ. He has passion to teach and grace to set order to things that are lacking.

God has gifted Isaac with an ability to stand back, discern what prophets and intercessors are doing in the broad picture, analyze what is happening through them and then exercise the self-discipline to organize his thoughts and put them into book form. This book is a great resource for all kingdom minded believers.

We are in such a pivotal time in church history. In the words of the great Charles Dickerson, "It was the best of times, it was the worst of times, it was the age of wisdom, it was the age of foolishness..." Apostle Isaac Watson has provided a book of wisdom that cuts through some of the foolishness taught regarding prophets and intercessors. I believe revelation is the key to authority. Prophetic revelation of scripture pours through Isaac Watson as he writes about the differences between prophets and intercessors. The insight in this book will give prophets the confidence to walk in their authority. This book provides a spiritual compass for proper placement of prophetic and intercessory gifts in the Body of Christ.

God is shaking everything that can be shaken. In the midst of the shaking, I believe God is realigning and redefining what it means to be an intercessor and a prophet in the 21st century. It is vitally important to be functioning in the right place in the body of Christ. Many are desperately searching for significance and grasping for their purpose in the plan of God. I say search no further. The wisdom and solid biblical foundation in this book is a great place to start. This book will serve as a plumbline. It will help measure you back to the purposes of God.

If you are reading these words, God is talking to you. Lean into the stirring of God through the pages of this book; and allow the Holy Spirit to educate, activate and empower your gifts.

Lean into the stirring of God through the pages of this book; and allow the Holy Spirit to educate, activate and empower your gifts.

Apostle Michelle McClain-Walters
Senior Leader, Overflow International Life Center
Best-selling Author, The Esther Anointing and
The Deborah Anointing

INTRODUCTION

I believe one of the greatest tragedies in the Church is the misplacement of gifts. Although biblical gifts of every kind are discussed, and clarity is brought through many books, articles, teachings, and the like, we still see a dilemma in the Body of Christ. As much as we know about the prophetic and its ministry, we still have people who are unwilling to embrace their calling as one.

This is not only because some people are afraid of what it means to be a prophet, but it is also because many are misinformed, misled, or misplaced. The ministry of the prophet has been under attack since its inception. Let's take a moment and explore when this attack began.

CAIN KILLED THE FIRST PROPHET

> *"Therefore the wisdom of God also said, 'I will send them prophets and apostles, and some of them they will kill and persecute,' that the blood of all the prophets which was shed from the foundation of the world may be required of this generation, from the blood of Abel to the blood of Zechariah who perished between the altar and the temple. Yes, I say to you, it shall be required of this generation."*
> *- Luke 11:49-51 (NKJV)*

The topic of prophets and intercessors is an ancient discussion that has been a continual conversation throughout the ages. It is one that extends all the way back to the garden of Eden. Abel, the son of Adam and Eve, who was killed by his brother Cain, is revealed to be the very first prophet.

Satan has been working tirelessly to assassinate the prophet's ministry and to defame its operation in the earth, but I believe God is bringing more clarity to what the new covenant prophet looks like. While the devil is trying to destroy this gift, I believe we are living in the days of the full restoration of its ministry.

Although the book of Genesis does not call Abel a prophet directly, Jesus calls him one. It is even stated that Abel was not only murdered as a man, but as a prophet. So from the time of the garden of Eden until now, the life of the prophet has been in danger.

After God created Adam He told him to rule and govern the earth. Within this commission was the mandate to be fruitful and multiply. As a sign of what God wanted to do in the earth, He gave Adam a prophet as a son. Abel represented the manifestation of God's prophetic purpose in the earth. When Eve gave birth to him, she not only gave birth to a baby boy, but to the prophetic plan of God. This was not by accident. It was always a part of God's plan for Adam and Eve to conceive and bring forth a prophet.

As part of Abel's prophetic assignment, he was a keeper of sheep by trade. He was the first shepherd named in the Bible. Sheep symbolically represent masses of people. Throughout scripture, they also represent the people of God. Abel's life was a picture of being called to shepherd people. Shepherds are given the responsibility to keep, instruct, anoint, protect, guide, correct, deliver, and carry their sheep into a safe place, so Abel's life signified a man called to bring people into safety, purpose, and fulfillment. This was Abel's prophetic destiny.

Unfortunately, his prophetic purpose never fully materialized. He never saw his potential manifest because his brother, Cain, murdered him due to envy and jealousy. This happened because Cain did not understand his own placement in the plan of God. He coveted his brother Abel, and instead of assisting him in his assignment, Cain ended up perverting his own.

"Now Cain talked with Abel his brother; and it came to pass, when they were in the field, that Cain rose up against Abel his brother and killed him. Then the Lord said to Cain, "Where is Abel your brother?" He said, "I do not know. Am I my brother's keeper?" And He said, "What have you done? The voice of your brother's blood cries out to Me from the ground. So now you are cursed from the earth, which has opened its mouth to receive your brother's blood from your hand."
- Genesis 4:8-11 (NKJV)

Cain was so consumed by Abel's relationship with God and God's favor towards him, that he began to mimic his brother. It was to the point that Cain began speaking to God as if he was the shepherd. After bringing an unacceptable sacrifice to God from the ground he tilled, he responded to God after killing his brother by asking, "Am I my brother's keeper?" He asked as if he was a shepherd and Abel was a lamb.

Symbolically, by killing his brother he killed a lamb whose life was acceptable to God. He prevented Abel's life from becoming an offering to God by taking it from him. Instead of tending to his brother to ensure he fulfilled his prophetic mandate, he murdered him and further sealed his own fate of damnation.

Cain was a tiller of the ground by trade. A tiller is a worker, bondman, or one who is in bondage to a work. Cain became a tiller of Abel's blood in the ground. Taking his brother's life enslaved him to his crime and perverted his purpose.

The story of Cain and Abel is symbolic of what God wants to do in the earth and how the devil does not want to see it get done. Prophets are important to God and because of that, the authenticity of their existence and influence will always be under attack. The kingdom of darkness will assassinate the prophetic seed and pervert purpose in order to prevent the promise from coming to pass.

One of the greatest ways the prophetic is perverted is through our own ignorance of what it entails.

***

THE IMPORTANCE OF INTERCESSORS

"Then the men rose from there and looked toward Sodom, and Abraham went with them to send them on the way. And the Lord said, "Shall I hide from Abraham what I am doing, since Abraham shall surely become a great and mighty nation, and all the nations of the earth shall be blessed in him?"

- Genesis 18:16-18 (NKJV)

"And the Lord said, "Because the outcry against Sodom and Gomorrah is great, and because their sin is very grave, I will go down now and see whether they have done altogether according to the outcry against it that has come to Me; and if not, I will know." Then the men turned away from there and went toward Sodom, but Abraham still stood before the Lord. And Abraham came near and said, "Would You also destroy the righteous with the wicked? Suppose there were fifty righteous within the city; would You also destroy the place and not spare it for the fifty righteous that were in it? Far be it from You to do such a thing as this, to slay the righteous with the wicked, so that the righteous should be as the wicked; far be it from You! Shall not the Judge of all the earth do right?"   *- Genesis 18:20-25 (NKJV)*

Throughout biblical history we see in the story of Abraham that he interceded for the city of Sodom.

This is the first record in the Bible of a man of God speaking directly to God on behalf of others. Abraham was an intercessor. Throughout his life and story we see him praying for the needs of others and partnering with God to bring His will to pass.

Abraham's relationship with God was unique and it teaches us something about the importance of intercession. When Abraham stood before the Lord on behalf of Sodom it was because a cry went out before the Lord from the people. That cry was for the judgment of God to be released upon the city of Sodom because of the perversion and injustice in the land.

There were rapes, murders, sodomy, and mistreatment occurring in that city and the people desired for the Lord to destroy them. God, hearing the cry, was going to visit that city in judgment, sparing no one. However, before doing this, God considered telling Abraham His plans. After doing so, Abraham was able to change God's mind. Although God destroyed the cities of Sodom and Gomorrah, He did hear Abraham's negotiation to spare the righteous.

The reason God listened to Abraham was because He knew Abraham carried the promise of greatness inside of Him. Abraham was called to bring change to the world and bless the nations through what he carried. Jesus ultimately was the fulfillment of the promises of God concerning Abraham's life.

This is the benefit of the called. Those who are in Christ carry the promise of the Father to bless nations through their lives. God still honors intercessors the way He honored Abraham.

These facts are indicators that the conversation about prophets and intercessors is not uncommon. As a matter of fact, these are two of the oldest subjects in the history of the Bible; and are the reason this book was written, to bring clarity to the subject of prophets and intercessors in a way that will enlighten the reader to be able to understand which of these two callings they are called to manifest. Not one of these graces is more important than the other. They both play a role in the Church to advance the Kingdom of God and to bring His presence and agenda to the earth.

I pray you are enriched with fresh understanding and revelation, and that you would be strengthened to stand in the grace God has called you to. I also pray that if you find that you are one who has been misplaced that you would have the courage to correct the misalignment and realign yourself with your true purpose. Let the journey into your prophetic purpose begin!

CHAPTER ONE
THE BLURRED LINES

We are living in a time where people are becoming more aware of their spiritual giftedness and are awakening to their God ordained purpose. The prophetic ministry is no longer a closeted ministry. There are more people prophesying today than we have ever experienced before.

We are also seeing more believers around the world being awakened to the mandate to pray and intercede. There is a charge in the Spirit, and a joy that is returning to the ministry of intercession. Many are answering the call and are responding to the mandate to pray. These are great advances in the Kingdom of God.

Jesus was both a Prophet and an Intercessor. His desire is to see both of these ministries fully restored in the earth. He also desires to see these ministries increase in their effectiveness and influence. In order to see this, there has to be a differentiation in the definitions and roles of both the prophet and intercessor. These graces, although similar in some ways, are very different in their make-up.

When not understood, the prophet and intercessor are often mistaken to take on the same role. This has caused many who function in one of these graces to believe they also most likely function in the other. There are many intercessors who through ignorance have believed themselves to be prophets because of this misunderstanding.

THE MISPLACEMENT

There are hundreds and maybe even thousands of prophets who are not aware that they have a prophetic career. Some of them are completely unaware of their mandate as a prophet because they were never identified as one. Due to various denominational barriers, doctrines, and ministry styles in the church, many people God has ordained to be prophets are only recognized as prayer leaders or intercessors. Again, this is not always intentional. Often times the church or organization the individual belongs to does not believe in prophets. As a result, every generation has a group of people who will live and die having never fully embraced their God ordained gifts and callings. This is a tragedy that I believe is being corrected as we become more aware of the knowledge of truth concerning God's plan for His Church.

What we believe about prophets and intercessors is directly connected to what we have been taught and observed. If you were raised in an environment where prophets led prayer meetings, unless there is teaching and understanding, someone could draw the conclusion that intercessors are prophets. Honestly, in many ways prophets and intercessors can look similar because both of these graces have prophetic responsibilities. There are, however, major distinctions between the two. I will take time to go through some of the similarities and distinctions in the chapters ahead, but it is important to note that you cannot conclude that someone is one or the other solely based upon the way a prayer meeting is led.

The line between the prophet and intercessor has

been blurred and it has become damaging to some. To be clear, both prophets and intercessors are necessary in the earth. What they are called to bring to humanity and the world is only intended to manifest the nature of Christ. However, here is the danger. It is never damaging for God's people to be called to prayer and intercession simply because all of God's people are called to pray. But it can be damaging for believers who are not prophets to falsely discern their place within the Body of Christ, and take on the responsibilities given to God-ordained prophets.

> *"So then, whoever eats the bread or drinks the cup of the Lord in an unworthy manner will be guilty of sinning against the body and blood of the Lord. Everyone ought to examine themselves before they eat of the bread and drink from the cup. For those who eat and drink without discerning the body of Christ eat and drink judgment on themselves. That is why many among you are weak and sick, and a number of you have fallen asleep. But if we were more discerning with regard to ourselves, we would not come under such judgment."*
> *- 1 Corinthians 11:27-31 (NIV)*

If there was a passage of scripture that motivates me the most in writing this book, this is it. What Paul explains here is very important and many believers overlook one of the things he is trying to reveal. This is not just about communion as a sacrament. There is a much deeper underlining message.

Paul admonishes the recipients of this letter who are

partaking in communion to first examine themselves. Growing up in church, I have always believed to examine yourself was primarily another way of saying, "Address any sin you may have in your life." In other words, the underlining message was if you have any sin in your life, repent first, and ask God for forgiveness. Then, after being cleansed, you become worthy to receive of the Body and Blood of Jesus through the taking of communion.

However, sin is not the topic of discussion in this message given by Paul. Repentance is not even mentioned in relation to examining oneself. So what was Paul doing? What was he revealing through these words concerning communion?

I believe Paul was addressing the importance of understanding why we do what we do. In the Corinthian church, many of them were eating of the bread and drinking of the wine excessively. They were no longer using this spiritual ritual in a spiritual way. They were using it as a way and excuse to simply eat and drink because they were hungry and thirsty.

They were eating "unworthily". In other words, they were eating in a way that was unintended by the Church. They were abusing the communion practice in order to feed their stomachs.

Paul was writing this to once again connect them with the true purpose of this sacrament. Communion was not only about the forgiveness of sin through the death of Jesus, it was also about the new covenant's power to rightly connect us in Christ. In other words, to examine yourself is not about sin in this context. It is about rightly discerning your place in the Body of

Christ. Paul is saying it is important to examine yourself with the Body of Christ in mind. Examine yourself as it relates to where you fit within the entire anatomy of the Body.

When you do not examine and rightly align yourself, you become susceptible to unnecessary attacks. Paul made this statement, ""*For those who eat and drink without discerning the body of Christ eat and drink judgment on themselves. That is why many among you are weak and sick, and a number of you have fallen asleep. But if we were more discerning with regard to ourselves, we would not come under such judgment.*"

What the apostle Paul is expressing here is huge. He is literally saying that there are people who are weak, sick, and have even died because they have not rightly discerned their place within the Body of Christ.

What I am about to say is very difficult to hear, but I believe there have been many people who have passed from this life prematurely because they have embraced a misplaced identity. There are some who have seemingly become fatigued and are constantly attacked in their health, energy, focus, and effectiveness after embracing an identity that may not be who they really are. I am not saying this is always the reason for fatigue, sickness, and premature death. But misplacement, according to Paul, does cause it and is worth examining deeper.

CULTURAL DIVIDE

The prophetic is an easy designation for misplacement simply because its implications can be vastly applied. For example, everyone is prophetic but not everyone is a

13

prophet. Everyone is called to hear the voice of God, but not everyone is called to equip other prophets.

Although there is a lot of information and revelation made available about the prophetic, there is still a lot to learn as far as being able to identify those who are simply prophetic from those who are called by God to be prophets. Some of today's leaders who have been recognized as prophets, both on a local and global scale, may be misplaced. Many of them are intercessors and not prophets.

Before I go further I want to make it clear that this book does not apply to every church everywhere. I do not claim to have an exclusive revelation. I know there are many churches around the world, some I know of and some I do not, that have beautiful, new covenant models, concepts, and paradigms in place that aid in them cultivating and developing healthy churches with a healthy culture, leaders, and believers.

I have seen successful prophetic schools modeled all around the world. Believers are being discipled in the love of God and are being trained in hearing the voice of God. The prophetic is becoming a normal part of the believer's life.

Prophets are also being educated on their role and responsibilities within the Church and the world. Many healthy prophetic voices are being raised up through what is called *schools of the prophets*. These are schools specifically designed for the equipping and education for the prophet's ministry. However, there are many initiatives that have been called schools of the prophets that are not schools of the prophets at all. They are simply schools that teach you about the prophetic, and there is a difference.

PROPHETIC ENVIRONMENTS

As a prophet it is very important to be found in the right environment. A prophet's calling and mandate requires a specific culture and atmospheres in order to be cultivated. Their maturing process is oftentimes a byproduct of these things. It is not enough to know about the prophetic. As a prophet, you must be placed in prophetic environments.

When prophets are not placed in the right environment the potency of their calling is likely to become diluted. They even risk forfeiting their prophetic purpose. Some may ask, "How can you forfeit your prophetic purpose? If they are called as a prophet how can they give that up?" The truth is, it can be forfeited by their choices. God calls you, but He does not make anyone respond with a "yes". God does not act against anyone's will. And your environment can either be a benefit or a hinderance to what you believe God has called you to do.

It is unfortunate how religion has attempted to suffocate the prophetic out of the Church. Many false accusations about the prophetic have made many people and churches reject its operation and renounce the movement of the prophetic as being insincere. This has become the case due to fear, ignorance, and the abuse of the prophetic. It is common for people to fear what they do not know or have not experienced for themselves. When prophecy is not balanced it can become spooky, weird, dominating, and out of order.

> *Let two or three prophets speak, and let the others judge. But if anything is revealed to another who sits by, let the first keep silent. For you can all prophesy one by one, that all may learn and all may be encouraged. And the spirits of the prophets are subject to the prophets. For God is not the author of confusion but of peace, as in all the churches of the saints."*
> *- 1 Corinthians 14:29-33 (NKJV)*

Paul had to address and bring order to the prophetic culture within the church of Corinth. Many of the believers who prophesied did not fully understand how the prophetic worked in a corporate environment, so they found themselves abusing it. As a result of this abuse, their culture became toxic. Toxic cultures influence and create toxic people.

Since there are many prophetic cultures that are seen and experienced as toxic, some churches would rather have nothing to do with the prophetic altogether. As a matter of fact, there are some churches that only see the prophetic as being a work of witchcraft and the occult because of the abuse they have witnessed and experienced.

Atmospheres and environments have the ability to create and to destroy. It is essential to be in a healthy prophetic culture if you are to develop into a healthy, Christocentric, new covenant prophetic believer. Here are 10 traits of a healthy prophetic culture.

- Prophetic cultures are motivated by love.

- Prophetic cultures create space for all to learn and grow in their gifts.

- Prophetic cultures encourage the plurality of gifts in the local church. No one person has the "it" factor.

- Prophetic cultures create space for people to make mistakes, learn, and grow without condemnation.

- Prophetic cultures identify Jesus as their standard and anchor for prophecy.

- Prophetic cultures encourage spontaneous songs, praise, hymns, worship, and minstrels.

- Prophetic cultures use prophecy as a tool to serve and assist one another in their journey with God, not as a way to manipulate or control people.

- Prophetic cultures are sensitive to the presence of God and are led in their gatherings by His voice.

- Prophetic cultures do not govern themselves. They submit to the government, order, and protocol of the local church leadership.

- Prophetic cultures have leaders that encourage the growth of the Body, and a Body that supports and aids in the health of one another.

CHAPTER TWO
BECOMING AN INTERCESSOR

"And God has appointed these in the church:
first apostles, second prophets, third teachers,
after that miracles, then gifts of healings, helps,
administrations, varieties of tongues. Are all
apostles? Are all prophets? Are all teachers?
Are all workers of miracles? Do all have gifts
of healings? Do all speak with tongues? Do all
interpret?" - 1 Corinthians 12:28-30 (NKJV)

One of the things I have heard over the years is not
everyone is an intercessor; and that there are certain
individuals with a gift of intercession which makes
their prayers more powerful, effective, articulate, or
authoritative. These characteristics are typically given to
those who are more encouraged to commit themselves
to the prayer ministry within the local church, or are
motivated to start their own prayer ministry.

In 1 Corinthians 12, Paul lists certain appointed gifts
and operations within the church. He makes it clear that
all of these gifts and operations are significantly essential
to the health and effectiveness of the church. He also
makes it clear that not everyone will be identified as one
of these gifts, and that no one will operate in all of these
gifts and operations.

Notice how "intercessor" is not listed in
1 Corinthians 12:28-30. It is not because the intercessor
is less important than the others named. I believe it is

because Paul cannot say about the intercessor the same thing he says about the others listed. Paul concluded the list with a series of questions. Are all apostles? Are all prophets? Are all teachers? And so on.

The answer to these questions is obviously "no". All are not apostles. All are not prophets. All do not speak with diversity of tongues. However, all can be intercessors. Therefore, the intercessor does not make this particular list.

Intercession is not something that is exclusively for special people within the church. Intercession is for everyone. It is not a gift, office, or mantle. It is a responsibility given to every born-again believer. Jesus is the Intercessor. He is the Mediator between heaven and earth. So, intercession is a position in Christ where spiritual transactions transpire between heaven and earth, and God and mankind, through the petitions of the saints.

Anyone can become an intercessor. As a matter of fact, God wills that you take upon the responsibility to pray. This is your inheritance and privilege as a son or daughter of God. As a son, you can speak to God and He will speak back. The Father's voice is the inheritance and right given to sons. This is what prayer and intercession is about. It is not about standing in an office. It is about lending your voice and influence to the world as a son of God.

***

GOD⬛ DIVINE MEDIATORS

One of the greatest joys a believer can experience in life is the fulfillment that comes from their prayer life. There is nothing like fulfilling pleasure that comes in knowing you are partnering with God and He is responding to your words as you are connected to His heart.

Since the intercessor both prays from their spirit and from the heart of God, there are prophetic responsibilities connected to their mandate. Praying from the heart of God involves hearing His voice and gaining an understanding of His will regarding a matter. This allows them to navigate in prayer according to what they feel God is doing and saying.

The ability to hear the voice of God for clear instruction and direction makes the intercessor prophetic. By developing a strong prayer life that is sensitive to God's voice, oftentimes strong prophetic utterance also becomes a part of the intercessor's ability. However, because of this, their primary job description is oftentimes confused as too many intercessors are misidentified as prophets.

For intercessors, if there is no clear defining language it can easily be misunderstood that they are called to be God's official spokespeople in the earth. In actuality, that is not the primary mandate or objective of what intercessors are called to be. Prophets are God's official spokespeople, not intercessors. Intercessors are, however, God's official mediators.

There is a difference between being a spokesperson and being a mediator. Being called as a mediator means you are given the primary responsibility of negotiation. All intercessors are called to negotiate. To negotiate means *to act as a link between two or more parties*. Intercessors are those who stand between heaven and earth and between God and mankind. This means that as an intercessor you are called to negotiate with God.

To negotiate also means *to dialogue between two or more parties in order to reach a beneficial outcome for the best interest of those parties*. So as an intercessor, you are given the responsibility of standing in the gap with the intentions of bringing about the best possible outcome in a situation. What is the best outcome? The will, plans, and purposes of God in the earth; the culture of heaven in the earth; and God's plans in the earth, including His plan of redemption and reconciliation for mankind. The intercessor has a role in these plans becoming a reality in the earth, so negotiation is very important when dealing with the realm of intercession.

> *"And the Lord said to Moses, "Go, get down! For your people whom you brought out of the land of Egypt have corrupted themselves. They have turned aside quickly out of the way which I commanded them. They have made themselves a molded calf, and worshiped it and sacrificed to it, and said, 'This is your god, O Israel, that brought you out of the land of Egypt!' " And the Lord said to Moses, "I have seen this people, and indeed it is a stiff-necked people! Now therefore, let Me alone, that My wrath may burn hot against them and I may consume them. And I will make of you a great nation."*

Then Moses pleaded with the Lord his God, and said: "Lord, why does Your wrath burn hot against Your people whom You have brought out of the land of Egypt with great power and with a mighty hand? Why should the Egyptians speak, and say, 'He brought them out to harm them, to kill them in the mountains, and to consume them from the face of the earth'? Turn from Your fierce wrath, and relent from this harm to Your people. Remember Abraham, Isaac, and Israel, Your servants, to whom You swore by Your own self, and said to them, 'I will multiply your descendants as the stars of heaven; and all this land that I have spoken of I give to your descendants, and they shall inherit it forever.' " So the Lord relented from the harm which He said He would do to His people. "   *- Exodus 32:7-14 (NKJV)*

In this dialogue between God and Moses, the children of Israel have been delivered from the hands of the Egyptians. They are waiting for Moses to come down from Mount Sinai where he was receiving instruction from God. It was during this time that Moses received the commandments given by God to the children of Israel.

The children of Israel were growing impatient as Moses was taking longer than expected with his meeting with God. As a result, the Israelites built a golden calf as an idol for them to worship. In a matter of days, they forgot who their Deliverer was and turned their affection to idols.

God, who witnessed Israel's impatience and unfaithfulness, was determined to destroy the entire nation. He proposed a new beginning for Israel with Moses being the new Adam, in a sense, and Moses' seed becoming the new line to inherit the promises of God. Listen to God's language in this dialogue.

> *"And the Lord said to Moses, "Go, get down! For your people whom you brought out of the land of Egypt have corrupted themselves."*
> *- Exodus 32:7(NKJV)*

God was so upset at this situation that He completely disowned the Israelites. He practically told Moses, "These are not My people. These are your people. I did not deliver them from Egypt. Moses, you have delivered them." In other words, God wanted absolutely nothing to do with Israel because of their rebellion and idolatry.

Moses, however, was able to do something many today would say is impossible. He was able to turn God's heart away from His wrath through intercession. The scripture says that Moses pleaded with the Lord. To *plead* in Hebrew means *to entreat the favor of.* Another definition is *to induce to show favor in place of wrath and chastisement.* To *induce* according to Oxford Languages means to *succeed in persuading or influencing to do something.* In other words, Moses was able to influence God to change His mind concerning Israel. And instead of wrath, God showed Israel mercy.

This is a powerful principle because it reveals that God can be influenced by our plea. Moses was able to influence God from destroying the children of Israel. Now, some would say that Moses was able to perform such a thing because he was one of the greatest prophets to ever live. However, Moses being able to influence God was not because he was a prophet. It was because he was an intercessor. In other words, it was not Moses the prophet standing before God. It was Moses the intercessor standing before God and influencing the outcome for the Israelites.

Many people are coveting to be a prophet because it is falsely believed and taught that prophets have the greatest connection with God. In actuality, the intercessor has the greatest connection with God. Being a prophet does not necessarily speak to closeness; and being aware of spiritual things does not correlate to knowing God's heart. The intercessor is the most closely connected to God, even moreso than prophets. This is why all prophets must first be intercessors.

As a mediator, Moses was able to negotiate with God in order to exchange His judgment for His favor and mercy.

"Then Moses pleaded with the Lord his God, and said: "Lord, why does Your wrath burn hot against Your people whom You have brought out of the land of Egypt with great power and with a mighty hand? Why should the Egyptians speak, and say, 'He brought them out to harm them, to kill them in the mountains, and to consume them from the face of the earth'? Turn from Your fierce wrath, and relent from this harm to Your people. Remember Abraham, Isaac, and Israel, Your servants, to whom You swore by Your own self, and said to them, 'I will multiply your descendants as the stars of

heaven; and all this land that I have spoken of I give to your descendants, and they shall inherit it forever.' " So the Lord relented from the harm which He said He would do to His people."   *- Exodus 32:11-14 (NKJV)*

Notice Moses' plea. He did not try to convince God to do anything based upon His own desires. He did not attempt to manipulate God in order to fulfill a selfish need. Moses understood something about God that ended up working in his favor. He understood that God always keeps His word. As a matter of fact, God magnifies His word even above His own name.

USE HIS WORD

"I will worship toward Your holy temple, And praise Your name For Your lovingkindness and Your truth; For You have magnified Your word above all Your name." - Psalm 138:2 (NKJV)

The name of God is to be honored and reverenced. Names are oftentimes intended to reveal natures and intentions. It is by the names of God that we see His nature revealed. Knowing the names of God is very important if you are to understand His heart.

There is, however, something this scripture reveals that God honors even more than His name. He honors His word. Psalm 138:2 says that God magnifies His word even above His name. This means that although God can do what He wills because He is God, what He wants to do is limited to what He says.

Moses understood this principle and used it to save the Israelites from God's wrath. Notice in Exodus 32:10, God says, *"Now therefore, let Me alone, that My wrath may burn hot against them and I may consume them."* God asked Moses to leave Him alone. This reveals that Moses standing in the gap between God and the Israelites as a righteous man was influencing God even though He desired to destroy them.

The declaration of the destruction of the Israelites was not a sure word. Moses' intercession was able to influence the outcome. Moses understood this and used one of the greatest tools in order to get God to change His mind. He negotiated with God by using God's own words.

> *"Remember Abraham, Isaac, and Israel, Your servants, to whom You swore by Your own self, and said to them, 'I will multiply your descendants as the stars of heaven; and all this land that I have spoken of I give to your descendants, and they shall inherit it forever.'" So the Lord relented from the harm which He said He would do to His people."*
> *- Exodus 32:11-14 (NKJV)*

One of the greatest things that can be said to God in prayer is, "God, You said!" Within the realm of prayer there are times when we express our hearts to God. There are also times when we are to express God's heart back to Him. This is done by reminding Him of His promises, meditating on His word, reviewing His faithfulness in times past, and as Moses does in this story, declaring His original intentions. God's original intent in Exodus 32 was for His promises to be fulfilled through the seed of Abraham, Isaac, and Israel. The promises were initially connected to Abraham and not Moses.

As an intercessor, Moses was able to put God in remembrance of what He had originally intended. He negotiated with God concerning Israel's future and a favorable outcome was decided. What we saw happen for Moses was not exclusive. Every intercessor is called to mediate and negotiate. As an intercessor, you have the responsibility to negotiate with God in order to enforce His will in the earth.

It is not that God does not want His will inaugurated in the earth. His desire is for His purposes to become the reality in our world. However, God's plan oftentimes requires the participation of mankind.

GOD'S SOVEREIGNTY

"The heaven, even the heavens, are the Lord's;
But the earth He has given to the children of
men."   *- Psalm 115:16 (NKJV)*

Yes, the heavens and the earth belong to God. Psalm 24:1 reveals that the earth is the Lord's and all of its fullness. However, in God's sovereign plan He delegated the earth to be stewarded by mankind. He has given the earth to the children of men.

This reveals the true authority given to the intercessor. Many of the negative things happening in the earth that are blamed on God may actually have nothing to do with Him. I have heard many people in grief from the loss of a loved one ask, "Why did God take them away from me?" It is very common to hear things said about God causing natural disasters; Him bringing devastation upon communities or nations and causing poverty, or marriages being broken up because it was not in His will. The blame game has been going on for ages wherein we see the sovereignty of God as the cause of much of humanity's pain and suffering.

The truth, however, is that God's sovereignty looks different than how many people project it. Sovereign is defined as *possessing supreme or ultimate power; a supreme ruler; an acknowledged leader; controlling influence; having supreme rank, power, or authority; supreme; preeminent; indisputable.* All of these definitions describe the sovereign characteristics of God, however, as the supreme and ultimate power He made the decision to give the earth over to man. This decision made by God has influenced the way He interacts with the affairs of the earth.

Since God gave the earth to men, even in His sovereignty He chooses to subject Himself to what He established. This means much of what God says and desires requires human obedience and subjugation to the will of God. God's will requires human partnership. Not because God is not sovereign, but because in God's sovereignty He decided to partner with man.

Intercession is man's partnership with God. Many calamitous events can actually be changed, redirected, cancelled, or in any other way affected when intercessors partner with God. Intercessors are the conduits of the mercy of God. Through their prayers, petitions, and activities, the destructive designs wrought through sin, rebellion, demons, and even natural means can be influenced by the Kingdom of God.

Not only are intercessors conduits of God's mercy, but they are also conduits of God's favor. When intercessors partner with God, favorable outcomes are the result. God's will to do good and to destroy the works of the devil both become a reality through the intercessor.

EMBRACE BEING AN INTERCESSOR

I believe there are a lot of people who believe they are prophets when in actuality they are intercessors. This truth does not demean who they are or demote them because they are not a prophet. In fact, I believe intercession is one of the most important graces within the Body of Christ.

It is only in, by, and through intercession that spiritual transactions can happen from heaven to earth, and from earth to heaven. I have seen where the intercessors in a church were almost treated like second-class citizens in the Kingdom, as if they are not God's negotiators. The mistreatment of intercessors is very sad to see. If people really understood the authority and privilege that comes with being an intercessor, more people would embrace this honorable calling and responsibility.

Sadly, because *intercessor* does not seem to be as much of a glorious title or position as *prophet,* many people run from it. This is only because many believers do not understand the role of the intercessor in the Kingdom of God. If they did, many of them would aspire to stand in this grace and use what has been given to them to change the world through the power of prayer.

To be clear, you can be both a prophet and an intercessor. This is not, however, the default design. Although intercessors and prophets share some of the same responsibilities in the Kingdom, being an intercessor does not make you a prophet. We will discuss some of the similarities and differences more throughout this book, but an easy way to look at how these two functions operate is by understanding that all prophets should be intercessors, but not all intercessors are prophets. And although all intercessors are not prophets, all intercessors have prophetic responsibilities.

CHAPTER THREE

PROPHETS: BORN AND BRED

Some of the most common questions I have received from people who are either curious or growing in the prophetic are these. How do you know if you are a prophet? And what is the difference between someone who is prophetic and someone who is a prophet?

If I were to define what a prophet is I would say a prophet is God's official covenant messenger and enforcer. They are also defined as God's official spokespeople. They enact and declare what the will of God is in the framework of His covenant with mankind.

One of the things that is important to understand when approaching the conversation concerning the calling of a prophet is that prophets are not made, they are born.

> *"Then the word of the Lord came to me, saying: "Before I formed you in the womb I knew you; Before you were born I sanctified you; I ordained you a prophet to the nations."*
> *- Jeremiah 1:4-5 (NKJV)*

God spoke to Jeremiah and told him, "Your prophetic calling was not your idea. It was Mine." This is significant because it reveals the origin of the call. You cannot make yourself a prophet. Likewise, no one can make someone else a prophet. It does not matter if they fast and pray. It does not matter if they receive the laying on of hands. Prophets do not receive their calling from man, but from God.

God made it clear to Jeremiah that the calling of a prophet does not begin in the natural. It is not something you come into after you are born. There are two words God used to describe the generative process of the prophet. He told Jeremiah that He **sanctified him**, and that He **ordained him**. Both of these things took place before God physically formed him. Sanctify comes from the Hebrew word qadash. Qadash means *to consecrate, to be holy, to dedicate, and to set apart*. Ordain comes from the Hebrew word nathan. Nathan means *to appoint, assign, fasten, and frame*. In other words, it is not the physical person who is sanctified and ordained as a prophet. It is the spirit of the person.

"And the spirits of the prophets are subject to the prophets." *- 1 Corinthians 14:32 (NKJV)*

What makes every prophet who they are is their spirit. Your spirit is what gives life to your soul and body. Genesis 2:7 says, *"And the Lord God formed man of the dust of the ground, and breathed into his nostrils the breath of life; and man became a living soul."*

The prophet's spirit is one in which God has dedicated, set apart, assigned, fastened, and framed uniquely in order for the individual to fulfill their assignment in the earth. All of the spiritual technologies necessary in order to fulfill their earthly assignment as prophets are given through their spiritual sanctification and ordination, so being a prophet is a divine calling and not an appointed office.

ALL PROPHETS ARE BORN

Being born as a prophet does not mean you will instinctively know this is your calling. In many cases, people do not know they are prophets early on unless they are bred in a church culture where the prophetic is emphasized. Within our local church, Encounter Worship Center, one of the things we initially provide for all of our new partners is personal prophetic ministry. After completing our new partners course, which is the introductory class into our personal church culture and vision, the graduates are prophesied over with their families.

During these times, even the children are able to receive what God is saying concerning their lives, potential, and future. Sometimes, God may even reveal callings, gifts, graces, personality and character strengths, and possible pitfalls to avoid in the future, among other things. This can aid a parent in understanding God's will and design for their children. If they understand God's heart for their children, then they can be more intentional in raising their children in the way they should go. This, of course, includes children with strong prophetic potential and children who may even be prophets.

Not every prophet is privileged to have this kind of prophetic breeding. Although the prophetic is becoming more common today, the majority of prophets do not come into the realization of their calling until later in life.

> *"Then Amos answered, and said to Amaziah: "I was no prophet, Nor was I a son of a prophet, But I was a sheepbreeder And a tender of sycamore fruit. Then the Lord took me as I followed the flock, And the Lord said to me, 'Go, prophesy to My people Israel.'" - Amos 7:14-15 (NKJV)*

At first glance, it appears as if Amos is saying one day he was not a prophet, then the next day...BOOM! God called him to be a prophet. But again, you have to remember that all prophets are born and not made. It does not matter your religious background, the type of family you were born into, your gender, or anything else. Either you are a prophet or you are not. Amos was not an exception.

In the context of this passage, Amos was not speaking concerning whether or not God called him as a prophet from birth. He was addressing the fact that he was not always called as a prophet by career. The context of his statement was concerning his livelihood and not his calling or spiritual makeup. He stated that he was a sheep breeder and a tender of sycamore fruit. In other words, Amos was speaking concerning how God has called him to change his careers from a breeder of sheep and agriculture into full-time ministry as a prophet.

Amos also stated that he was not a son of a prophet. It is important to note that he was not speaking of his relation to his natural father or to whoever was responsible for raising him as a child. The term *sons of the prophets* was commonly understood in Amos' day. *Sons of the prophets* in the Old Testament were those who were a part of the training schools for ministry or what have been commonly referred to as *schools of prophets*. Biblically and historically, if you were a part of the school of the prophets you were considered one of the sons of the prophet. We will cover this topic exclusively in a later chapter.

Amos is not referring to his home training or upbringing. He is stating that prior to now he has had no official training in the prophet's educational program. Amos was saying that his prophetic call did not come from man. He was not raised to follow the ways of a prophet. He had no formal introduction into a prophetic career nor did he receive any official training. The Lord simply took him one day. God commissioned him to change careers, embrace a new livelihood, and walk fully in his prophetic purpose and calling.

IT WILL BE REVEALED

"For you have heard of my former conduct in Judaism, how I persecuted the church of God beyond measure and tried to destroy it. And I advanced in Judaism beyond many of my contemporaries in my own nation, being more exceedingly zealous for the traditions of my fathers. But when it pleased God, who separated me from my mother's womb and called me through His grace, to reveal His Son in me, that I might preach Him among the Gentiles, I did not immediately confer with flesh and blood, nor did I go up to Jerusalem to those who were apostles before me; but I went to Arabia, and returned again to Damascus.
- Galatians 1:13-17 (NKJV)

I absolutely love these words by Paul concerning his own calling as an apostle. Although the calling of a prophet is being discussed in this book, Paul's writing concerning his apostleship can also be applied to the calling of a prophet.

As it has been stated earlier, all prophets are born. Paul says that God separated him from his mother's womb and called him through His grace. This correlates with the words of the prophet Jeremiah who expresses how God knew him before He formed him in his mother's womb. This reveals that nothing has changed from the Old Covenant to the New Covenant. In the same way all prophets were born before the New Covenant was instituted, that same pattern remains consistent concerning ministry gifts after the New Covenant and the Church were put into place.

Although all prophets are born, there are many prophets who do not know they are prophets. Sadly, some live their lives without ever coming into the full knowledge of their calling. Others come into the knowledge of their prophetic calling later in life. I believe Paul gives an explanation as to why these things happen.

Paul says that it was the predetermined plan of God to reveal His Son in him. The word *reveal* in verse 16 is derived from the Greek word apokaluptó. Apokaluptó means to uncover, bring to light, reveal, make plain, manifest, or unveil. It means to reveal what is hidden or what was previously not made known. Who you are called to be and what you are called to do in most cases are not immediately known. These things are oftentimes revealed over a period of time. So although someone may be born a prophet, that revelation may not become obvious to that person until later in life.

How do you know whether or not you are called to be a prophet? You will know because it will be revealed to you. As I have stated earlier, no one can make someone a prophet. However, the calling of a prophet can be revealed either to the person directly or to someone else concerning them.

CAN I GET A WITNESS?

I believe there will be several types of witnesses who will serve as affirming and confirming agents. First and most importantly, there should always be the witness of God. If you are called to be a prophet then surely this truth will be revealed by God to you over time. One of the reasons why there is so much misplacement in the Body of Christ is because there are many people who have accepted an identity God did not personally speak to them about. They have allowed others to project an identity upon them and have adopted it as their own.

To be clear, I do not believe God will always be the first one to speak directly to the person concerning their own calling. This brings us to the next type of witness. God will always reveal the calling of a prophet through other people. God uses trustworthy believers of good reputation to reveal truth, revelation, and insight concerning lives, journeys, assignments, callings, and mandates. This means prophetic insight is not only confirming.

I have heard many leaders say that prophecy should only confirm what God has already spoken to you about. This is not always true. Although many prophecies will confirm what God has already previously declared in the earth, there are also times when God will speak something new into the earth. There will be times when God will declare new things to people that they have never heard or thought of before. These manifestations display the creative, as well as the revealing prophetic nature of God.

God can and does speak prophetically through people you may not know in order to reveal His purposes for your life. However, I have learned that identifying graces and callings are better received and are considered more trustworthy when they are done by those in which there is genuine relationship and accountability.

Of course, this is not easily portrayed when you

believe you may be a prophet, but you are not around prophetic believers or leaders. If your church culture does not believe in prophets of course they will not be able to identify a prophetic gift. When this is the case it is more common for God to speak through strangers or prophetic ministers who are outside of your immediate circle of influence. However, when your relationships and accountability understand the prophetic, it should be easier for them to identify it upon your life. They are able to see your lifestyle, passions, grace, fruit, and character.

This leads us into the third witness that is given, which is fruit.

> *"Therefore by their fruits you will know them."*
> *- Matthew 7:20 (NKJV)*

Your fruit speaks of your nature. It represents your innate ability to produce what is natural to you. Some things are more natural to some people than others. One of the best ways to identify what you are called to is to examine what comes easily or natural for you. The prophetic is no different, especially when you were born to be a prophet. One of the ways God reveals this to you is by having you examine the fruit of your life.

In the prophet's life, there are typically signs from childhood that can point to this calling. These signs become evident even before coming into the knowledge of Christ. Signs such as meaningful dreams, visions, foreknowledge, godly wisdom, reoccurrences, prophecy, words of knowledge (knowing facts about people, places, situations, etc. supernaturally), encounters with angels, demons, and other spiritual beings, sensitivity to spiritual realities, a zeal for justice, righteousness, and truth, among other things.

Although this list is not exhaustive, many of these signs will be extremely evident. The prophet's spirit is what makes many of these signs innate, so the prophet's life will produce this type of fruit.

The witnesses given are not in any specific order. However, it is dangerous to fully embrace a calling or identity without receiving revelation from God yourself concerning it. This calling is spiritually discerned and spiritually revealed. Even if being a prophet is not revealed to you first, it should be revealed from God to you at some point. Otherwise, there may be grounds to reconsider whether you were rightly identified or possibly misplaced.

It is also dangerous to fully embrace a calling or identity without the wisdom of trusted voices, leaders, and accountability. I have seen and known many people stubbornly declare, "I know what God showed me or told me," and do not look for insight or wisdom from others concerning it. If God has truly called you to it, there will be confirming words concerning it from others who also know the voice of God.

To believe you alone have full rights or ultimate knowledge concerning the plan of God for your life is to be deceived and to become an island unto yourself. This kind of behavior can lead you into living from a place of self-righteousness, special knowledge, and a lack of genuine accountability.

This is not how the Church is designed to operate.

Whenever you are looking to gain understanding concerning the plan of God for your life, whether it be for direction, relationships, or identifying what you are called to be and do, the greatest posture to have is one of humility and accountability; and over time, God's plan will be revealed to you.

CHAPTER FOUR

THE MISCONCEPTION: I HAVE A PROPHETIC GIFT

"Pursue love, and desire spiritual gifts, but especially that you may prophesy."
- 1 Corinthians 14:1 (NKJV)

Of all the spiritual gifts mentioned in scripture, prophecy is the most talked about. The apostle Paul, who authored two-thirds of the New Testament, wrote more about prophecy and the prophetic than any other gift. His discourse on the prophetic alone in 1 Corinthians 14 is almost two times longer than his entire letter to Philemon, so the prophetic was undoubtedly important to Paul and required clarity concerning its administration.

One of the greatest misconceptions I have witnessed from intercessors is the idea that having a strong and accurate prophetic gift must make you a prophet. Unfortunately, many prophetic people have taken on false identities because of the lack of clarity on the difference between prophets and those who operate in revelatory gifts. Revelatory gifts are gifts in which hidden things regarding a matter are revealed. Paul mentions some of them in 1 Corinthians 12.

There are diversities of gifts, but the same Spirit. There are differences of ministries, but the same Lord. And there are diversities of activities, but it is the same God who works all in all. But the manifestation of the Spirit is

given to each one for the profit of all: for to one is given the word of wisdom through the Spirit, to another the word of knowledge through the same Spirit, to another faith by the same Spirit, to another gifts of healings by the same Spirit, to another the working of miracles, to another prophecy, to another discerning of spirits, to another different kinds of tongues, to another the interpretation of tongues. But one and the same Spirit works all these things, distributing to each one individually as He wills.
- 1 Corinthians 12:4-11 (NKJV)

In Paul's list of spiritual manifestations, he mentions several gifts of revelation which include the word of wisdom, word of knowledge, prophecy, discerning of spirits, different kinds of tongues, and the interpretation of tongues. These gifts are all revealing in nature. Without being exhaustive, I want to define each of these manifestations in order to bring understanding to how individuals with these abilities may be misidentified as being prophets.

WORD OF WISDOM

The word of wisdom also known as the message of wisdom is a gift of instruction. This manifestation speaks into what you are to do with what is to come. This gift is not, however, simply foretelling. It is also directional in nature.

It is often stated that wisdom is the proper application of knowledge, so the word of wisdom is knowing what to do with what you know. It is revealing what is to come, but it is also revealing instructions concerning what is to come.

WORD OF KNOWLEDGE

This spiritual manifestation is also known as a message of knowledge. It is a message to a recipient, which reveals current or past information or facts. It is intended to speak into present and past situations. What makes the word of knowledge different than the word of wisdom, is the word of wisdom speaks into your future, while the word of knowledge speaks into your past and present.

What many may assume is prophecy in operation, may actually be the word of knowledge in operation. When names, phone numbers, addresses, past or present scenarios and situations are revealed, it is not prophecy being manifested. It is the word of knowledge being revealed.

PROPHECY

Although prophecy is expressed through foretelling and forth-telling, I do not believe that prediction alone is prophecy, nor is the predictive nature of prophecy its primary operation. I believe that more importantly than prediction, prophecy is speaking and expressing the heart, mind, and purposes of God in the earth. What is the purpose of prediction if God's heart is not being portrayed? Prophecy can occur through word, song, writing, poetry, dance, musical instruments, art, drama, demonstration, among other things.

DISCERNING OF SPIRITS

The discerning of spirits is the ability to sense into the spirit world. Through this spiritual manifestation, the motives, driving forces, and transactions of the spirit world are revealed. It is through the discerning of spirits that angels and demons are discerned, and the invisible realm becomes more clear. The intentions and motives of people are also revealed through this manifestation.

The discerning of spirits can often reveal what is driving or motivating someone to do what they are doing or be the way they are. This gift does not only manifest through seeing. It can manifest through any or all of your senses. In other words, you can see, smell, taste, hear, feel, and sense what may be occurring in the spiritual realm.

DIFFERENT KINDS OF TONGUES

Different kinds of tongues also known as the diversity of tongues or languages must not be confused with the believer's prayer language. There is a difference between the two. The diversity of tongues is the ability to speak in a language, either of natural or spiritual origin, in which the speaker has never naturally learned.

The manifestation of this gift may require the interpretation of tongues in order for the hearers to be edified. The partnering of these two gifts is what makes them revealing in nature. The diversity of tongues operate in multiple facets. A message can be released through this gift, which requires interpretation because it is either a spiritual language or unknown language by both the speaker and the hearers. There are also times where no interpretation is needed because although the speaker may not naturally understand the language, it is spoken in the language of the hearers and they understand.

INTERPRETATION OF TONGUES

The interpretation of tongues is the manifestation of the spirit which compliments the diversity of tongues. It is the supernatural ability to understand what was previously spoken in an unknown language. Through this grace, either unlearned natural languages or spiritual languages can be interpreted.

Notice this manifestation is called the interpretation of tongues and not the translation of tongues. In other words, this gift essentially does not serve as a strict, word for word translation of a language whether natural or spiritual. It is instead an interpretation which gives the essence of a message. The interpretation of a spiritual message can be revealed as a revelation, prophecy, knowledge or word of knowledge, and even teaching.

"But now, brethren, if I come to you speaking with tongues, what shall I profit you unless I speak to you either by revelation, by knowledge, by prophesying, or by teaching?"
- 1 Corinthians 14:6 (NKJV)

***

THE GIFTS ARE FOR EVERYONE

When the apostle Paul reviewed these gifts in 1 Corinthians 12, he was not describing the gifts of the prophet. He was describing the gifts of the Spirit. In other words, being able to operate in these revelation gifts is the manifestation of being filled with the Holy Spirit. It is not the manifestation of standing in the ministry gift of prophet.

These gifts are not intended for only some believers. It is actually the will of God for every Spirit-filled, born again believer to flow in all of these gifts. This is one of the reasons why intercession is important. The more you engage with God and spiritual affairs, the more the spirit world opens itself up to you. When you begin to embrace the mandate of prayer and intercession these gifts begin to become active in your life.

The gifts of the Spirit, particularly the revelatory gifts, all make up the prophetic realm. So when we are dealing with words of wisdom, for example, we are dealing with the prophetic realm as one of the manifestations of the Spirit. Paul admonishes the church to desire spiritual gifts, especially prophecy. This indicates that the grace to prophesy and the prophetic realm is not reserved only for certain people in the church. Quite the contrary. The prophetic realm is reserved for anyone who desires to operate in it.

I have met many believers who believe prophecy is not their "gift". This belief gives them the impression that they are to leave the prophesying to those who have that gift. The problem I have with this is that the manifestation of the Spirit has been given to each person individually so that all may profit. Paul went as far as to say that God works all in all.

> *"And there are diversities of activities, but it is the same God who works all in all."*
> *- 1 Corinthians 12:6 (NKJV)*

He did not say that He works some in all. Paul could even have said that God works all in some. The emphasis was that He works all in all. In other words, all of the gifts are for everyone. Every believer should live a prophetic lifestyle.

PRAYER CULTIVATES YOUR PROPHETIC POTENTIAL

> *"Therefore let him who speaks in a tongue pray that he may interpret."*
> *-1 Corinthians 14:13 (NKJV)*

One of the things I love about this verse is that it reveals the power of prayer. The writer says that the one who speaks in a tongue is to also pray that he interprets. This alludes to the idea that while you may be operating in one gift, prayer can unlock another in your life. In other words, prayer has the ability to expand your prophetic expression.

Spirit led prayer leads you into a life in the Spirit. It opens you up to the spiritual world. This is the power of intercession. As a mediator, not only do you share in and experience this earthly realm, but you also share in and experience the heavenly realm. God invites you into His world.

If you are an intercessor, you are called to live a

prophetic life. This is why many intercessors believe they may be prophets. As an intercessor you have access to the prophetic. Not only do you speak to God, but God also speaks to you. Not only do you bring the affairs of the earth to God's attention, but God also makes you aware of heavenly realities. This transaction is intended to bring you into more effectiveness as an intercessor.

In prayer, God may give you a word of knowledge concerning a person or situation in order for you to pinpoint your prayer assignment. There may be times while praying in the Spirit that God may give you the interpretation of your tongues in the form of a prayer direction. God may even cause you to discern a situation or root cause to a dilemma in order for you to address it through your intercession. This reveals that one of the ways the gifts of the Spirit are cultivated and strengthened is through your prayer life.

It is not uncommon for intercessors to develop a strong prophetic desire and unction. Many intercessors assume that because their prayers are prophetic, and they prophesy and minister through revelatory gifts they must be prophets. This is mainly due to the lack of language concerning what prophets are mandated to do besides prophesy. The effects of this lead many intercessors down a road of looking to be identified as prophets. Not only does this happen, but through ignorance, leaders and other members in the Body of Christ may also mislabel them.

The reality is having a prophetic gift does not make you a prophet, neither does being able to call out the details of someone's life. It simply means you operate in the word of knowledge, and not everyone with this gift is a prophet. Although prophets are known for moving and operating in revelatory manifestations, these things should not be the totality of what they are known for. There are other responsibilities that prophets have besides prophesying that we will cover in the next chapter.

I want to encourage you to continue to grow in your gifts. Grow in prayer and allow God to strengthen the spirit of revelation in your life. It is ok to be gifted. You should not feel pressured to be anything other than who God has called you to be. Your gifts are not your identity. Your gifts are given as tools in order for you to influence your world with Heaven's reality.

CHAPTER FIVE

PROPHETIC RESPONSIBILITIES

As mentioned previously, one of the reasons there is so much confusion regarding intercessors being identified as prophets is because both of these graces have prophetic responsibilities. There are a lot of misplaced gifts because of what intercession unlocks. Many believe that because they are able to access the spiritual realm with a great degree of spiritual activity manifesting, they must be a prophet. But there are several responsibilities given to both prophets and intercessors, and determining if you are a prophet cannot be measured by these responsibilities alone. Every intercessor and prophet has the responsibility to:

1. Pray

2. Shamar or Discern

3. Prophesy

4. Minister through the revelation gifts

Although prophets are known for these responsibilities, intercessors are given these responsibilities as well. The reality is that intercession is a key to heavenly transactions, so these alone cannot determine whether or not someone is a prophet. We discussed the revelation gifts in the previous chapter, so I will take time in this chapter to cover the other three responsibilities.

RESPONSIBILITY TO PRAY

Intercession is one of the primary responsibilities of every believer, especially prophets and prophetic people. Being an intercessor is different than someone who simply says they pray to God. Many people pray only to get their personal needs met, but an intercessor lives to lay down their own life for others.

Intercessors do not only pray what is on their heart. They pray with an ear to God's heart. They surpass the place of routine and ritualistic prayer and move into prophetic intercession. Prophetic intercession is when your intercession is driven by what God reveals to you. Through this type of intercession your revelation gifts are involved in your prayers. You intercede based upon what you may discern, words of knowledge or wisdom you may receive, prophetic insights, or even tongues and interpretation of tongues.

> *"Now Jacob went out from Beersheba and went toward Haran. So he came to a certain place and stayed there all night, because the sun had set. And he took one of the stones of that place and put it at his head, and he lay down in that place to sleep. Then he dreamed, and behold, a ladder was set up on the earth, and its top reached to heaven; and there the angels of God were ascending and descending on it."*
> *- Genesis 28:10-12 (NKJV)*

"Jesus answered and said to him, "Because I said to you, 'I saw you under the fig tree,' do you believe? You will see greater things than these." And He said to him, "Most assuredly, I say to you, hereafter you shall see heaven open, and the angels of God ascending and descending upon the Son of Man." - John 1:50-51 (NKJV)

It is revealed through scripture that Jesus, the Son of Man, is the ladder Jacob dreamt about. He is the point of divine transfer, interaction, and transaction between heaven and earth. Since the ladder stood between heaven and earth it is also a prophetic picture of the intercessor. It represents Jesus the Mediator and all those who access the throne of grace through His life as High Priest.

"Seeing then that we have a great High Priest who has passed through the heavens, Jesus the Son of God, let us hold fast our confession. For we do not have a High Priest who cannot sympathize with our weaknesses, but was in all points tempted as we are, yet without sin. Let us therefore come boldly to the throne of grace, that we may obtain mercy and find grace to help in time of need." - Hebrews 4:14-16(NKJV)

Intercession is what invokes the activity of angels and releases supernatural breakthrough and miracles. This is important to understand because when engaging in intercession we are not only commissioned to engage within the affairs of the earth, but the affairs of the spirit realm as well. This is one of the reasons why the revelation gifts become more alive in the lives of believers. Everything that is necessary in order to be successful concerning spiritual affairs is made manifest to those who will give themselves to prayer.

This is why effective prophets must first be intercessors. The fact of the matter is that all prophets should be intercessors. If a prophet's commitment is not first to intercession, I would not listen to them. Prophets must be measured by their prayer lives.

This is important because the prophet's spirit is fashioned to connect to spiritual channels. In other words, prophets are innately sensitive to the spiritual realm. This is not only limited to connecting with God. The spiritual realm is not a Christian concept alone. Someone being able to sense into the spiritual realm does not mean they are hearing or sensing from God. The spiritual realm consists of both light and darkness and the prophet's prayer life is what keeps them connected to the life of God.

PROPHETS AND INTERCESSORS: STEWARDSHIP IN PRAYER

As you grow and mature in the prophetic, one of the things you will learn to discern is what to do with what God reveals. Prophetic people have the responsibility of knowing and discerning what God is saying to them and what to do with what they hear. Should you release what was revealed to you to the Body of Christ and to creation in general by way of prophesying it, or should you release what you heard back to God by way of intercession? Some things God will speak to you so that you can speak it right back to Him. He leads you in prayer and intercession; and one of your responsibilities is to learn how to follow.

One of the ways God trains you in the prophetic is by giving you responsibilities to steward in prayer. Immature prophetic voices have little restraint over what they say, and always look for opportunities to prophesy and say what they know. Although prophecy is godly, it is something that has to be stewarded well. Not everything God shows you should be publicly revealed to others.

There are many times where God will reveal something to you only for it to be echoed back to Him. This is one of the purposes of prophetic intercession. Because God gave the earth to mankind, His will requires our partnership.

"In this manner, therefore, pray: Our Father in heaven, Hallowed be Your name. Your kingdom come. Your will be done On earth as it is in heaven." - Matthew 6:9-10 (NKJV)

Jesus told His disciples to pray for the Father's kingdom to come and will to be done on earth as it is in heaven. If God's will could not be affected by our prayers, then why would Jesus instruct His disciples to specifically pray in this manner? Evidently, your prayers can usher in the will of God and invite His purposes into the affairs of man. God knows this and does not leave His intercessors guessing concerning what His will is. He understands that the key to much of what He desires to release in the heavens and in the earth is in your mouth, so He speaks to you and looks to see what you will do next.

This also pertains to dreams and visions. Not

every dream is intended to be turned into a prophetic declaration. Many dreams and visions are given to you as prayer assignments. Always take your God-given dreams to prayer. This is one of the ways you become a better steward over the mysteries of God.

In times of intercession, He is moved by those who are moved by Him, so it is imperative that you learn how to follow Him. Once He hears us echo His words and heart back to Him, it gives Him permission to release what He has already settled in His heart concerning His purposes.

RESPONSIBILITY TO SHAMAR

"By a prophet the Lord brought Israel out of Egypt, And by a prophet he was preserved."
-Hosea 12:13 (NKJV)

In the verse above, the word *preserved* is the Hebrew word *shamar*. The word shamar means to keep, watch, protect, preserve, put a fence around, encircle, seal a hedge, or build a wall of protection. It describes the protective responsibility of the prophet or intercessor. I have heard a lot of emphasis on it being the responsibility of prophets to shamar, but intercessors also have this responsibility.

"I have set watchmen on your walls, O Jerusalem; They shall never hold their peace day or night. You who make mention of the Lord, do not keep silent, And give Him no rest till He establishes And till He makes Jerusalem a praise in the earth." - Isaiah 62:6-7 (NKJV)

The word shamar is also translated as watchman. Watchmen in ancient Israel were positioned on watchtowers or high walls and were responsible for warning the city in which they were stationed of impending danger or attack. Demonic attack, schisms, and spiritual warfare arise in every church, family, community, and individual's life. When watchmen take responsibility to guard and protect, many of these attacks are prevented, nullified, or made void.

Through the discerning of spirits hidden motives and schemes are made known. Intercessors are able to pinpoint the source of demonic attack. Strategies can be made in order to seal up breaches and hedges which can represent broken covenant relationships, lies, accusations, financial discrepancies, divisions, and systematic frailties within the church, among other attacked and weakened areas. Intercessors and prophets are repairers and are called to repair such breaches.

Those who are called to shamar are called to preserve. To preserve means *to keep from harm, damage, danger, or evil.* It also means *to protect or to save.* Churches, communities, and families can suffer unnecessary warfare and attacks when the shamar aspect of the prophetic is not understood or enforced.

> *"Then the Lord God took the man and put him in the garden of Eden to tend and keep it."*
> *- Genesis 2:15 (NKJV)*

God told Adam to tend and keep the garden he was placed in. The word used for *keep it* is shamar. God told Adam to shamar the garden. The shamar aspect of the prophetic also speaks of a gardening function. He was to tend to the garden in the sense of caring for it how a gardener would tend to his garden. The same word is also used for shepherds who are called to tend and keep their sheep.

SHEPHERDING PROPHETS

Prophets and shepherds are oftentimes seen completely separate. However, shamar prophets can also be shepherding prophets. They can be prophets who are called to keep, tend to, protect, and preserve.

One of the Hebrew words for prophet is *roeh*. Roeh is translated as seer. It is believed that the word roeh is connected to the Hebrew word rohi, which means shepherd, and is one of the names of God. This would mean that prophets and seers have a shepherding dimension to them. This reveals that prophets are not only concerned about prophesying, but protecting and preserving as well.

RESPONSIBILITY TO PROPHESY

This responsibility is probably the biggest source of misplacement. Within the church there are many people who are recognized as prophets solely based upon the strength of their ability to prophesy. If they consistently give accurate prophetic words, can sing prophetically, pray prophetically, or have an accurate word of knowledge it is likely that someone will identify them as a prophet. The fact of the matter, however, is that every believer is given grace to live a supernatural lifestyle.

It is erroneous to determine whether or not someone is a prophet solely upon the observation of them knowing how to prophesy. Although prophets have a responsibility to prophesy, so do intercessors. The gift of prophecy is not only given to prophets, but to those who are filled with the Holy Spirit. The manifestation of the Spirit is given to every Spirit-filled believer.

Prophetic intercessors oftentimes develop a mature gift of prophecy through their experience with God in prayer. There are many times as an intercessor that God will have you to prophesy in your times of prayer through decrees, declarations, and prophetic acts. Prophecy is not only speaking, but also expressing the heart, mind, and will of God, so it is not uncommon for prophetic intercessors to be given instructions to perform prophetic dramatizations. These acts or expressions can include writing, drawing, dancing, shouting, clapping, bowing, praying in specific places, facing a particular direction while praying or prophesying, among many other things. God oftentimes trains you to hear His voice through your obedience to His instruction even if it seems foolish.

"You also, son of man, take a clay tablet and lay it before you, and portray on it a city, Jerusalem. Lay siege against it, build a siege wall against it, and heap up a mound against it; set camps against it also, and place battering rams against it all around. Moreover take for yourself an iron plate, and set it as an iron wall between you and the city. I Set your face against it, and it shall be besieged, and you shall lay siege against it. This will be a sign to the house of Israel. "Lie also on your left side, and lay the iniquity of the house of Israel upon it. According

to the number of the days that you lie on it, you shall bear their iniquity. For I have laid on you the years of their iniquity, according to the number of the days, three hundred and ninety days; so you shall bear the iniquity of the house of Israel. And when you have completed them, lie again on your right side; then you shall bear the iniquity of the house of Judah forty days. I have laid on you a day for each year."
- Ezekiel 4:1-6 (NKJV)

Ezekiel was instructed by God to lay on his left side for many days. He was then instructed to do the same thing on his right side as he was to prophesy against Jerusalem. This was a prophetic act and picture which allowed Ezekiel to experience to some degree God's perspective in how He saw Israel in that day.

Even as a prophet, Ezekiel was acting as an intercessor so that the Israelites could see God's judgments and patience through his prophetic dramatization. I am sure Ezekiel felt strange carrying out these instructions, however, God used this prophetic act to test his obedience and strengthen his prophetic trustworthiness. Prophets and intercessors will experience similar testing. It won't necessarily be to the extent of what Ezekiel endured, but they will be tested nonetheless. This is necessary because God desires to know His prophetic people will be both obedient and trustworthy. By giving them prophetic responsibilities, including the mandate to prophesy, it gives them opportunity to develop an ear for His heart.

Intercessors who have developed a passion for prayer will also develop a burden for people which makes you more empathetic, sensitive, and aware of their needs. You will not only pray what you know about them from common knowledge, but you will also feel God's heart concerning them which makes you more open to minister prophetically to them.

Prophecy alone must not be the determining factor as to whether you are called to be a five-fold gift, specifically a prophet. Prophets are mandated to do much more than prophesy. I will explore some of these mandates in the next chapter.

CHAPTER SIX

TAKE YOUR CUE FROM THE NEW

I have witnessed the prophetic ministry bless many people around the world.

I have witnessed the power of the prophetic word break the power of addiction. I have also witnessed God open the hearts of sinners and cause them to want to embrace Jesus because of a prophecy they received. Prophecy continues to bring healing to the lives of those who are physically afflicted, and emotionally and mentally unwell, and it gives direction to those who are lacking it. The prophetic ministry is an amazing tool in the hands of those who have the right idea concerning it.

I make this point because although I have seen the wonders of prophecy, I have also witnessed the abuses of prophetic ministry. Prophecy itself is a tool. Depending on who has this tool will also determine how it is used. There are many who use prophecy for their own selfish gain. There are also those who are abusive when ministering prophetically because of wrong doctrine.

Doctrine is defined as *a belief or set of beliefs held and taught by a Church, political party, or other group; Teachings or something taught as the principles or creed of a religion or belief system.* Doctrine is important. It determines the lens in which you see the world. It also determines what you believe about God, people, and yourself. If your doctrine is wrong it can have a negative impact on the way you minister to and treat people. This is why it is important to understand what the foundation of all prophecy is.

> *"But what did you go out to see? A prophet? Yes, I say to you, and more than a prophet. For this is he of whom it is written: 'Behold, I send My messenger before Your face, Who will prepare Your way before You.' "Assuredly, I say to you, among those born of women there has not risen one greater than John the Baptist; but he who is least in the kingdom of heaven is greater than he."* **- Matthew 11:9-11 (NKJV)**

John the Baptist was said to be the greatest of all old covenant prophets. There was no one else born of a woman that was greater than he was in that day. He was the prophet mandated to prepare the way for Jesus, the coming Messiah. Yet, Jesus declared that those who are in the Kingdom of God are even greater than John. Those who are least in the kingdom of heaven are those who have believed the Gospel of Christ. These are they who have become partakers of the new covenant. This is why those who have believed Jesus' words are greater than those who have believed John's words. John's words pointed to life, while Jesus' words are life.

John was the last of the old covenant prophets, when a new covenant was on the brink of unfolding. This is significant for us to understand because we are all now ministers of the new covenant, which means our model of ministry is different than John's or any other old covenant prophet.

YOUR MODEL MATTERS

What Jesus provided through His covenant with the Father was not just forgiveness of sins for us. He also provided a new model for ministry.

> *"God, who at various times and in various ways spoke in time past to the fathers by the prophets, has in these last days spoken to us by His Son, whom He has appointed heir of all things, through whom also He made the worlds; who being the brightness of His glory and the express image of His person, and upholding all things by the word of His power, when He had by Himself purged our sins, sat down at the right hand of the Majesty on high, having become so much better than the angels, as He has by inheritance obtained a more excellent name than they."*
> *- Hebrews 1:1-4 (NKJV)*

> *"The Son radiates God's own glory and expresses the very character of God..."*
> *- Hebrews 1:3a (NLT)*

> *The Son is the dazzling radiance of God's splendor, the exact expression of God's true nature—his mirror image!*
> *- Hebrews 1:3a (TPT)*

Jesus is said to be the brightness of God's glory and express image of His person. He expresses the very character of God, the true nature of God, and is even said to be the mirror image of God. In other words, if you want to know what God is like, how He feels, what He thinks, or how He would respond, you should not look to the old covenant prophets. You look at Jesus. John the Baptist only had the prophets of old to look to for his example. We have Jesus the Prophet as our model.

> *"But now He has obtained a more excellent ministry, inasmuch as He is also Mediator of a better covenant, which was established on better promises. For if that first covenant had been faultless, then no place would have been sought for a second." - Hebrews 8:6-7 (NKJV)*

The Old Covenant was faulty. It was not the best representation of the heart or nature of God. It was made for the people because of their pride and their inability to progress in faith. They needed written laws in order to understand righteousness, and even with their laws their understanding was skewed.

Prophets are God's covenant messengers. They are called to declare, defend, and enforce God's covenant. This is performed mostly through their words and actions depicting God's intentions, standards, promises, and consequences for either obeying or disobeying His covenant agreement and its conditions. It was based upon works and obedience; blessings and curses. In other words, if you obeyed the instructions of the covenant you would be blessed. If you disobeyed or did not fully carry out its conditions, you would be cursed.

This was the standard and model for old covenant prophets. They ministered and prophesied through the lens of this covenant. Do not consider this a bad thing because during those times that was the covenant God was faithful to; and as long as you are faithful to what God is faithful to, you are considered righteous. The question now is, which covenant is God faithful to?

The author of Hebrews says that Jesus has obtained a more excellent ministry, and that the New Covenant was instituted because the first one was not faultless. The word faultless in the Greek is defined as *blameless, free from defect, or irreproachable*. In other words, the first covenant was defective in that it could bring reproach upon God's name. It did not reflect the true nature of God.

When prophets minister from the lens of the first covenant their message could bring a reproach upon God's name. Not because God never used it, but because it is now obsolete.

"In that He says, "A new covenant," He has made the first obsolete. Now what is becoming obsolete and growing old is ready to vanish away." - Hebrews 8:13 (NKJV)

The word used for obsolete is the Greek word *palaioó*. It is defined as old, worn out, decayed, made wax, not recent, ancient, or antique. The first covenant has been deemed outdated by God, and a better covenant has been created.

Jesus is the Mediator of this better covenant. He becomes the new standard for prophecy and the prophetic ministry. As a prophetic believer, your lens has been upgraded and your model has been perfected.

Although the prophets of old had amazing ministries in which we can all learn and be encouraged from, they are not your model. You no longer measure your standard with their words or ministries alone. Jesus' standard becomes your model example.

> *"Now it came to pass, when the time had come for Him to be received up, that He steadfastly set His face to go to Jerusalem, and sent messengers before His face. And as they went, they entered a village of the Samaritans, to prepare for Him. But they did not receive Him, because His face was set for the journey to Jerusalem. And when His disciples James and John saw this, they said, "Lord, do You want us to command fire to come down from heaven and consume them, just as Elijah did?" But He turned and rebuked them, and said, "You do not know what manner of spirit you are of. For the Son of Man did not come to destroy men's lives but to save them." And they went to another village."*   *- Luke 9:51-56, NKJV*

This is one of my favorite examples of how Jesus' ministry is displayed as a superior model than that of the prophets of old. In this story, Jesus is on His way to Jerusalem and passes through Samaria. The Samaritans refused to accommodate Him while He was there because they were not the center of His attention at this point. He was not staying in the village of the Samaritans in order to minister to them. He was simply passing through.

In response to the Samaritans refusing to receive

Jesus, His disciples, James and John wanted to destroy the entire city by calling down fire from heaven upon them. This desire did not originate from their own hearts. This idea was adopted from the prophet Elijah's ministry within their Old Testament scriptures.

> *"So Elijah answered and said to the captain of fifty, "If I am a man of God, then let fire come down from heaven and consume you and your fifty men." And fire came down from heaven and consumed him and his fifty. Then he sent to him another captain of fifty with his fifty men. And he answered and said to him: "Man of God, thus has the king said, 'Come down quickly!' " So Elijah answered and said to them, "If I am a man of God, let fire come down from heaven and consume you and your fifty men." And the fire of God came down from heaven and consumed him and his fifty."*
> *- 2 Kings 1:10-12(NKJV)*

Elijah was a prophet known for his demonstration of the power of God. He was confrontational, governmental, and had a miraculous ministry. He called down fire upon these men in order to prove his ministry as God's true prophet. These acts brought great fear upon these men as well as judgment upon King Ahaziah.

James and John looked to reenact this scene from the days of Elijah in order to make an example out of the Samaritans. What is interesting, however, is Jesus' response to their desire. He did not tell them, "It is written. Do unto them as Elijah has done unto Ahaziah's army." Although Elijah's example was permissible in his day, it was unacceptable according to Jesus' model.

Jesus told James and John, "You do not know what manner of spirit you are of." In other words, they were operating from the wrong spirit. Their prophetic lens was through the eyes of Elijah instead of through the eyes of Jesus. New Covenant ministry is a ministry of life and not death. Jesus saw the Samaritans according to the covenant God was creating through Him. The disciples saw the Samaritans through the lens of the law of Moses. It is important that you have the right lens because when your lens is wrong your prophetic ministry can be damaging.

THERE IS A DIFFERENCE

I have heard many people say there is no real difference between old covenant prophets and new covenant prophets; that their ministry and mission are the same. However, I believe there is a difference. When the new covenant was instituted through the birthing of the Church, the mandate of the prophet also went through changes. But before the changes are laid out, here are some of the things that remained the same.

Firstly, prophets are still only called by God. Secondly, you still cannot become a prophet. Prophets are born and the spirit of a prophet is still what makes you one. These things remain consistent and true from the old to the new covenant. This is important to understand because no amount of prayer can make someone a prophet. Neither does a licensing, commissioning, or ordination certification. You either are or you are not, and that is determined by God's preordained purpose for an individual. Now that we know some of the things that remain the same, it is imperative for not only prophets, but all believers to know what changed within the prophet's ministry.

The first thing that changed is the covenant the prophet is faithful to and enacts. Prophets are to be faithful to whatever covenant God is faithful to, and God is faithful to the new covenant. The old covenant concerns God's law given to Moses. The new covenant concerns God's law given to Jesus Christ.

Salvation and reconciliation to God are the fruit of the ministry of Christ. Jesus declared that the Son of Man did not come to destroy men's lives but to save them, so prophetic ministry should be salvific in nature. This is a different ministry than what the old covenant presented. The old covenant was based upon obedience, disobedience, works, blessings, and curses. Relationship was not the goal of the old covenant. The works of obedience unto righteousness were. If obedience could not be wrought then judgment and curses would be the result.

To be clear, God is still a righteous Judge. There are still consequences to sin and disobedience.

"For the wages of sin is death, but the gift of God is eternal life in Christ Jesus our Lord."
- Romans 6:23 (NKJV)

Sin leads to death regardless of your covenantal lens. However, Jesus came as the solution to sin, and prophetic ministry modeled after Christ should always lead to life. So prophecy which involves correction, judgment, direction, rebuke, and repentance is relevant and necessary, but it should never lead to condemnation or death.

One of the purposes of new covenant prophecy is to convict the hearers. Conviction and condemnation are not the same thing. They can look similar, but are very different in nature. Condemnation inflicts your conscience with guilt and shame. It tells you that you deserve punishment, and it crushes your hope of changing. Conviction, on the other hand, is designed to bring to light or expose wrongdoings, feelings, or thinking in order for you to correct them. Conviction brings you to a place of accountability and to an awareness of the grace of God which empowers you to change.

I believe all new covenant prophecy, regardless of its intention, depth, tone, or specificity, should have three elements. It should always manifest what I call the Three R's. Prophecy should always be *redemptive, restorative, and reconciling* in nature. Let me define these three natures.

Redemptive: *Acting to save someone from error or evil.*

Restorative: *To give back someone or something that was lost or taken; To return someone or something to its original state; To put or bring something back into existence or use; To return something to an earlier or original condition by repairing it or cleaning it.*

Reconciling: *To reestablish a close relationship, as in marriage; To become compatible, harmonious, or consistent; To settle or resolve.*

It is not enough to point out problems and highlight the darkness. What is God saying about the darkness, problem, sin, or dysfunction? Jesus came to redeem, restore, and reconcile us to the purposes, promises, and person of God.

The second thing which changed is that prophets are no longer isolated in the name of being consecrated to God. Under the old covenant, prophets mostly worked alone. If Israel was rebellious the prophets kept their distance in order to declare God's judgments and mercy without being associated with the nation's transgression. Under the new covenant, they are now planted within the Church and sent from the Church, which is the Body of Christ.

"Now you are the body of Christ, and members individually. And God has appointed these in the church: first apostles, second prophets, third teachers, after that miracles, then gifts of healings, helps, administrations, varieties of tongues." **- 1 Corinthians 12:27-28 (NKJV)**

Paul declared that God has appointed prophets in the church. To appoint is defined as *to establish, set, fix, place, put, plant, or purpose.* This implies that prophets must intentionally be established within the church. This does not only relate to prophets being a part of the global church, but they should also be planted within a local church. One of the definitions for *appointed* is *purposed.* God has purposed prophets within the church, which means prophets who are isolated from the church are outside of their purpose.

Notice, Paul did not say that these gifts and operations are appointed or established in the marketplace, government, education, entertainment, or any other cultural institution. He said they are established in the church. The church is their base. It is where they are to reside, learn, influence, and grow in their purpose.

This does not mean that prophets or other gifts cannot be called to influence cultural institutions or the mind molders of society. However, these secular institutions must not be their base or place of initial appointment. Prophets are planted within the church to first influence the church, and they are secondarily sent to influence society.

The third thing that changed is the focus of their prophetic ministry. Under the old covenant the people relied on the prophet to hear from God. Under the new covenant, the prophet teaches the people how to hear from God for themselves.

"But two men had remained in the camp: the name of one was Eldad, and the name of the other Medad. And the Spirit rested upon them. Now they were among those listed, but who had not gone out to the tabernacle; yet they prophesied in the camp. And a young man ran and told Moses, and said, "Eldad and Medad are prophesying in the camp." So Joshua the son of Nun, Moses' assistant, one of his choice men, answered and said, "Moses my lord,

forbid them!" Then Moses said to him, "Are you zealous for my sake? Oh, that all the Lord's people were prophets and that the Lord would put His Spirit upon them!"
- Numbers 11:26-29 (NKJV)

Joshua wanted Moses to prevent Eldad and Medad from prophesying because from Joshua's perspective it would make Moses look bad. Moses understood that the plan of God has always been to have a people unto Himself who would hear His voice and speak for Him on their own regardless of what camp they are a part of. Moses responded and said his wish was that all of God's people were prophets and carried His Spirit.

God did not make all of His people prophets. However, He did make a way for everyone within the church to be filled with Holy Spirit who is also the prophetic Spirit. This is significant because Moses' ministry represented an old covenant paradigm where the entire nation of Israel depended on his relationship with God. Today, each one has their own relationship with God through Jesus Christ, so prophets are no longer the only bearers of God's voice. They are called to do more than prophesy. New covenant prophets are now also called to create prophetic cultures within the context of the church by raising up prophetic people.

The prophet under the new covenant is different from the prophet under the old covenant in this regard. Old covenant Israel was reliant upon the prophet to speak to them on God's behalf. Only the prophet was trusted to carry the Word and instruction of the Lord to the people. The people felt they were too weak, sinful, and unworthy to speak to God for themselves. They were afraid to speak to God, let alone on God's behalf. Old covenant prophets were the only ones worthy enough to be trusted to carry the Word of the Lord as God's covenant messengers. Under the new covenant, the prophet takes on a slightly different role.

IT IS IN THEIR NATURE

Although the prophet is still trusted to prophesy and express God's heart to the church and nations, they are also responsible for reproducing themselves and imparting their prophetic nature into every believer within the church. Prophets within the church are no longer prophesying and creating a dependency from the people upon themselves for all prophetic ministry. They are teaching the church how to hear from God and how to release what He is saying into the earth.

The prophetic is not just a function. It is a nature. Simply getting around prophets will activate the prophetic in your life. The role of prophets is to release their nature so that they are not the only ones who are prophetic within the church. Prophets are commissioned to play their part in creating a prophetic church.

This means they not only teach the saints how to hear God and prophesy, but they also teach believers how to live by every word that proceeds out of the mouth of God. The church is taught how to live life sensitive to the voice and presence of God. The life of the prophet is intended to model what it looks like to live a prophetic lifestyle which every believer should strive for.

Prophets impart what is on their lives by getting

involved in the life of the church. They not only prophesy to the church, but they teach, train, equip, and release those within the church into their own unique, prophetic journey and sphere of influence. If you are called to be a prophet, then you are called to get involved in the life of believers in order to create in them a stronger prophetic nature. Being prophetic should not happen by accident. It is through the influence of prophets that intentional prophetic growth within a church community is initiated, so every prophet has the capacity and responsibility to govern and cultivate the life of the church.

This means prophets should not only be able to prophesy, pray, operate in the gifts of the Spirit, and cast out demons. These things are not enough to prove a prophetic career. Everything mentioned is simply Christianity 101. Prophets also have the responsibility of cultivating a prophetic community with what they carry within their lives.

CHAPTER SEVEN
PROPHETIC SCHOOLS

"For you can all prophesy one by one, that all
may learn and all may be encouraged."
- 1 Corinthians 14:31 (NKJV)

As the prophetic is becoming more common throughout the Body of Christ, one of the major focuses and points of demystification revolves around the prophetic training processes of the church. As we have learned throughout this book, it is God's will for every believer to prophesy. The church itself is designed to speak and express the heart, mind, and will of God. It is not the responsibility of prophets alone.

WHY THE MISPLACEMENT?

I believe there are more people within the church who are intercessors that have been misplaced as prophets, than there are true prophets that have only been identified as intercessors. This is not an uncommon dilemma. The misplacement of these callings is mainly due to the way we educate the church concerning prophetic operations.

The church has done an amazing job at educating believers about the prophetic as well as teaching how it is God's will for them to prophesy. However, throughout the years there has been little effort towards creating language that distinguishes between prophetic believers and actual prophets. The overemphasis of everyone being prophetic without explaining the distinct descriptive responsibilities given to prophets has created a blurring of the lines between the two.

I believe wholeheartedly in equipping believers to understand how the prophetic should be a normal part of their Christian life. There should be discipleship, education, training, resourcing, and the placement of believers both within the church and within their given spheres of influence. However, in order to do these things more effectively I believe many of our schools and training initiatives need to be reset and recalibrated.

LET☒ PRESS THE RESET BUTTON

If there is to be a greater measure of effectiveness in the way the prophetic is presented and received, it has to begin with our language. Language can either be a connector or it can be a barrier. It can either bring clarity or breed more confusion. The way something is articulated matters. Much of the confusion within the prophetic occurs because of the language the church uses.

The school of the prophets is one of the initiatives the church needs to revisit. I believe in schools designed for the development of prophets, however many of the schools today actually have nothing to do with prophets. If there has ever been anything that is diluting to the genuine calling of prophets, it is what has been adopted as schools of the prophets. What I have witnessed around the world pertaining to these schools is not all bad, however, there are some things we need to press the reset button on.

I am not on a campaign for cancelling schools of the prophets. I believe in them and believe they are important. I am only suggesting that there needs to be a redefinition given to many of these schools. Much of what has been called schools of the prophets are really prophetic schools that are intended for all believers. There is a difference between the two. Prophetic schools are designed for the prophetic development of Christians, whether they are a prophet or not. These schools are intended to educate the general body of Christ on the responsibility given to every believer to be prophetic.

Although prophets can and often do participate in these prophetic schools, typically they are given the opportunity to learn and grow among companies who simply desire to understand and operate in the prophetic. Prophetic schools are not necessarily designed for prophets to learn the full scope of the responsibilities and mandates given to them.

WHAT ARE PROPHETIC SCHOOLS?

Prophetic schools are intentional learning environments where what it looks like to be a prophetic culture is explored both in theory and practice. These schools typically will cover in various levels of depth one or several subject matters. These subjects may include topics such as prayer and intercession, hearing the voice of God, personal prophecy, corporate prophecy, dreams and visions, scribing, prophetic song, minstrels, prophetic dance, and gifts of the Spirit, among other things. The goal of many prophetic schools is to teach the foundational aspects of the prophetic. They are also designed to teach the importance of the prophetic within the church and life of the believer.

These schools not only educate in classroom format, but they are also intended to get believers to see their own prophetic potential and to move in prophetic expression themselves. Again, I do not want to overgeneralize prophetic schools. Many schools are able to inspire those who have never prophesied before as well as challenge those who may be more experienced in the prophetic. One of the more effective training initiatives for these schools is taking believers through a series of prophetic exercises or activations.

YOU CANNOT TEACH HOW TO PROPHESY

One of the things I want to make clear is that these exercises or activations are not hocus pocus, nor are they tricks or formulas that give people supernatural information or knowledge. Prophetic exercises are about getting people to rely on their relationship with God. You cannot teach anyone how to prophesy, but you can guide them in understanding how God speaks to them.

> *"And it came to pass at that time, while Eli was lying down in his place, and when his eyes had begun to grow so dim that he could not see, and before the lamp of God went out in the tabernacle of the Lord where the ark of God was, and while Samuel was lying down, that the Lord called Samuel. And he answered, "Here I am!" So he ran to Eli and said, "Here I am, for you called me." And he said, "I did not call; lie down again." And he went and lay down. Then*

the Lord called yet again, "Samuel!" So Samuel arose and went to Eli, and said, "Here I am, for you called me." He answered, "I did not call, my son; lie down again." (Now Samuel did not yet know the Lord, nor was the word of the Lord yet revealed to him.) And the Lord called Samuel again the third time. So he arose and went to Eli, and said, "Here I am, for you did call me." Then Eli perceived that the Lord had called the boy. Therefore Eli said to Samuel, "Go, lie down; and it shall be, if He calls you, that you must say, 'Speak, Lord, for Your servant hears.' " So Samuel went and lay down in his place. Now the Lord came and stood and called as at other times, "Samuel! Samuel!" And Samuel answered, "Speak, for Your servant hears."
- 1 Samuel 3:2-10 (NKJV)

Although the Lord was calling Samuel and speaking with him, he did not know how to identify His voice. Samuel had a similar issue that many people have today. He did not know how to distinguish between God's voice and man's voice. Every time God called him, he ran to Eli mistaking his voice for God's.

Eli instructed Samuel on hearing the voice of God. He taught him how to discern the difference between the Lord speaking to him and other voices speaking to him. Eli's only job was to guide Samuel in trusting his relationship with Him. Everyone hears God differently because God does not speak to everyone the same way. Eli perceived that God was speaking to Samuel in a particular way and he led him to trust God's voice.

Like Eli, prophetic schools are given as guides to get believers to trust how God speaks to them. Whether it be through visions and imagery, an audible voice, journaling, or dreams, once you learn how God speaks to you, expressing what He is revealing is how you move from hearing from Him to prophesying for Him.

CHAPTER EIGHT

SCHOOL OF THE PROPHETS

"Now the sons of the prophets who were at Bethel came out to Elisha, and said to him, "Do you know that the Lord will take away your master from over you today?""
- 2 Kings 2:3 (NKJV)

"Then Elijah said to him, "Stay here, please, for the Lord has sent me on to the Jordan." But he said, "As the Lord lives, and as your soul lives, I will not leave you!" So the two of them went on. And fifty men of the sons of the prophets went and stood facing them at a distance, while the two of them stood by the Jordan."
- 2 Kings 2:6-7(NKJV)

"A certain woman of the wives of the sons of the prophets cried out to Elisha, saying, "Your servant my husband is dead, and you know that your servant feared the Lord. And the creditor is coming to take my two sons to be his slaves.""   *- 2 Kings 4:1(NKJV)*

"Then Saul sent messengers to take David. And when they saw the group of prophets prophesying, and Samuel standing as leader over them, the Spirit of God came upon the messengers of Saul, and they all prophesied."
                                    - 1 Samuel 19: 20(NKJV)

Before exploring how the school of the prophets relates to the church today, I would like to briefly give historical background on its biblical context and significance. Samuel, Elijah, and Elisha led prophetic companies and assemblies in which those who were a part were called sons of the prophets. The actual assemblies themselves have been coined by many as schools of the prophets. In those day these schools were dedicated to the development of budding prophets.

Within the school, students would not only learn about prophecy, but would also become educated on the history of God's journey with Israel, as well as other significant cultural elements such as their music, languages, arts, and sciences. During these times, there were no seminaries for those who were interested in becoming Jewish scholars, so the schools of the prophets accommodated both prophets and those who were interested in learning their spiritual history so that they could teach it to their generation and descendants. These schools were groundbreaking because they created a safe haven for potential leaders and prophets to be groomed as well as have a community in which they can view as family.

FROM THE CAVE TO THE COMPANY

"So it was, when Elijah heard it, that he wrapped his face in his mantle and went out and stood in the entrance of the cave. Suddenly a voice came to him, and said, "What are you doing here, Elijah?" And he said, "I have been very zealous for the Lord God of hosts; because the children of Israel have forsaken Your covenant, torn down Your altars, and killed Your prophets with the sword. I alone am left; and they seek to take my life." Then the Lord said to him: "Go, return on your way to the Wilderness of Damascus; and when you arrive, anoint Hazael as king over Syria. Also you shall anoint Jehu the son of Nimshi as king over Israel. And Elisha the son of Shaphat of Abel Meholah you shall anoint as prophet in your place. It shall be that whoever escapes the sword of Hazael, Jehu will kill; and whoever escapes the sword of Jehu, Elisha will kill. Yet I have reserved seven thousand in Israel, all whose knees have not bowed to Baal, and every mouth that has not kissed him."
- 1 Kings 19:13-18 (NKJV)

The prophet Elijah was in a very low place. He was running for his life, hiding in a cave because the prophets were being killed by the children of Israel. He knew that they were also in pursuit of him. Within this cave, Elijah had an encounter with God that changed his life and his assignment.

Elijah thought he was the only prophet left; as if the

children of Israel had killed the rest of them off. God gave him a reality check. He asked Elijah, "What are you doing here?" In other words, this cave is not a part of your calling. God literally needed Elijah to repent and change the way he thought.

Elijah walked alone. He was isolated. He clearly had knowledge of other prophets in his day, but there was no indication that he had relationship with any of them. It is easy to understand how Elijah felt he was God's last living hope, however, he was quite possibly relationally challenged. God enlightened his eyes and gave him a new paradigm and assignment.

He was instructed to anoint Elisha as prophet in his place. In other words, he was told to disciple Elisha, a young man, who would be doing exactly what God had anointed him to do. God concluded His word to him by stating that there were seven thousand other prophets that had not bowed to Baal.

What God was doing to Elijah was breaking the spirit of isolation off of him. I believe it was in this cave that Elijah received revelation about developing his company of prophets. God told Elijah in so many words, "Look around. You are not the only one. There is prophetic potential all around you in prophets you currently may not know; and these prophets simply need development." What Elijah did not see developed around him, God was mandating him to raise up.

SCHOOL OF THE PROPHETS TODAY

Today, schools of the prophets, although found within the scriptures, are actually more rare than prophetic schools. These schools are not created for the general Body of Christ. They are intended specifically for the development of prophets. Within these schools, prophets are taught, trained, developed, recognized, and deployed. Their mission is to raise up, cultivate, educate, and give experience to prophets, both to those who are emerging in their identity, as well as those who are established.

What makes the school of the prophets different from prophetic schools is its exclusivity. These schools should be reserved for those who are believed to be prophets. If someone believes they are a prophet, is recognized as one, or is recommended because an authority sees prophetic potential, it may be suggested that they go through one of these schools. Within these schools the prophet's grace is studied, along with their strengths, weaknesses, burdens, and make-up; and the history and origin of the prophet's ministry.

Schools of the prophets go beyond teaching the basic fundamentals of prophetic ministry. They are not solely about equipping everyone to prophesy and understand the mystical realm. There is also an emphasis on societal impact as prophets. There is a need to understand how prophets use their influence, grace, and knowledge to impact the spheres of culture they have been called to engage. These schools are designed to advance prophets into the full thrust of their ministry. This is what causes schools of the prophets to stand out from prophetic schools.

The school of the prophets is not so much about prophecy and prophesying, as it is about understanding the full measure and mandate of the prophet's ministry. It is about exploring the specific responsibilities of the prophet's career and learning how to apply them in a practical way. Due to the lack of true schools of the prophets, many of today's prophets are only measured by the accuracy of their prophetic words, even though prophets are called to do much more than prophesy.

DON'T JUST PROPHESY, BUILD!

"Then the prophet Haggai and Zechariah the son of Iddo, prophets, prophesied to the Jews who were in Judah and Jerusalem, in the name of the God of Israel, who was over them. So Zerubbabel the son of Shealtiel and Jeshua the son of Jozadak rose up and began to build the house of God which is in Jerusalem; and the prophets of God were with them, helping them." - Ezra 5:1-2 (NKJV)

Haggai and Zecharaiah revealed a very important aspect of the ministry of the prophet. Although they prophesied to the Jews, their work did not end with their words. They did not prophesy, then tell the leaders to take the word and figure it out themselves. Ezra says that Haggai and Zechariah were with them, helping them build. In other words, these prophets not only prophesied, but they partnered with the Jewish community and leadership in working towards their vision to rebuild the house of God in Jerusalem.

One of the major characteristics and responsibilities of new covenant prophets is that they are called to partner within the church as builders. Ezra reveals how the prophet's hands are just as valuable as their words. This is an important concept because it places greater emphasis on how prophets are to relate to people. We covered how once the covenants changed from the old to the new, prophets also moved from isolation into community. With this change also came the duty to strengthen God's vision by strengthening God's people.

To build is defined as *to establish and develop over a period of time.* Haggai and Zechariah were given the assignment to help build the house of God in Jerusalem. This is a picture of what prophets are called to do today. However, instead of building a physical house of God, prophets today are called to establish and develop strong prophetic believers.

> *"Now, therefore, you are no longer strangers and foreigners, but fellow citizens with the saints and members of the household of God, having been built on the foundation of the apostles and prophets, Jesus Christ Himself being the chief cornerstone, in whom the whole building, being fitted together, grows into a holy temple in the Lord, in whom you also are being built together for a dwelling place of God in the Spirit. "*
> *- Ephesians 2:19-22 (NKJV)*

The church has now become the house of God. It is no longer a literal building, but physical people who are the dwelling place of God. Every vision given to the church, whether it is a local church or the global church, is purposed to increase the knowledge of Christ within people and regions. Prophets work with and within the church not only through prophesying, but also through teaching, networking, preaching, discipleship, training, consultation, prayer, team development, and vision strategizing with leadership.

Although the responsibility to prophesy should never be diminished, it is only a fraction of what prophets are called to do. Due to the reality that many ministries and books written about the prophetic have been based solely on the charismatic nature of the prophet, we have limited our scope concerning prophets to simply having charisma, and the prophet is so much more than that.

> *"Now Judas and Silas, themselves being prophets also, exhorted and strengthened the brethren with many words. And after they had stayed there for a time, they were sent back with greetings from the brethren to the apostles. However, it seemed good to Silas to remain there. Paul and Barnabas also remained in Antioch, teaching and preaching the word of the Lord, with many others also."*
> *- Acts 15:32-35 (NKJV)*

Judas and Silas stayed in Antioch in order to exhort and strengthen the believers there. The emphasis and nature of their stay was because they were prophets. As prophets, the resources they carried were necessary for that church at that time. They were not just having church services in Antioch. It was not an evangelistic three-day revival featuring the prophets Judas and Silas, where they traveled back home after the weekend festivities.

The scripture says that they stayed there for a time. In the Greek, the word used for *stayed there* is *poiēsantes.* This word is defined as *committed.* In other words, Judas and Silas committed to the church in Antioch for a time. They committed to this church's vision. They committed to encouraging and challenging the believers there. And this commitment could have been for weeks, months, or even years. Another definition for the word *poiēsantes* is to *construct.* These two prophets were committed to constructing the believers for a time. Their energy was not only on giving encouraging prophecies, but on developing a strong church. They were there to exhort and strengthen the church.

Exhortation includes but is not limited to prophesying. To exhort is to be positioned to pull people into place. It literally means to pull, draw, exhort, beckon, plead with people, or pull them into position. This involves more hands on engagement with the church and believers than simply speaking a prophetic word over them. Prophets are called to adjust the saints. They are mandated to cultivate the church's prophetic potential and mature them in living soberly as believers. This requires prophets to be placed and identified not only by their charisma, but by their capacity to build, exhort, and strengthen.

Schools of the prophets focus on many of these dynamics. Each prophet has their own strengths and weaknesses and these schools help to identify them in order for them to be most effective in their calling. I believe the equipping of prophets has to be done intentionally. There are several things prophets must understand while embracing the full measure of their purpose.

It is important for prophets to understand how to partner with churches and assist in their development, health, and growth. They must learn how to create and develop teams and spiritual companies. They must learn how to interact as ambassadors or delegates before leaders within the church as well as around the world; and they have to learn how to operate and relate within their own local church while serving under senior leadership and amongst co-laborers. As schools of the prophets evolve and become more exclusive for the development of prophets, I believe the rewards will become evident. This evidence will be clearly seen not only in the life of the prophets, but within the church as well as through the impact left within their given spheres of influence.

CHAPTER NINE

WHERE DO I FIT?

I want to revisit Paul's words to the Corinthian church.

> *"So then, whoever eats the bread or drinks the cup of the Lord in an unworthy manner will be guilty of sinning against the body and blood of the Lord. Everyone ought to examine themselves before they eat of the bread and drink from the cup. For those who eat and drink without discerning the body of Christ eat and drink judgment on themselves. That is why many among you are weak and sick, and a number of you have fallen asleep. But if we were more discerning with regard to ourselves, we would not come under such judgment."*
> *-1 Corinthians 11:27-31 (NIV)*

God is concerned about your placement. He has designed for you to operate within the Body of Christ in a specific way. You are designed to carry out specific assignments and mandates. And when you do not discern your design and placement, it can be damaging.

For some of you, God is giving you courage to walk in your God-given identity. Whether that means coming into the revelation and embracing that you may be a prophet or that you are a true prophetic intercessor who through the lack of language and blurring of lines embraced being a prophet. Wherever you find yourself, it takes courage to embrace the true purposes of God for your life.

In his letter to the Corinthians, Paul says that there is a risk in not embracing the true purposes of God. He declared that there are consequences that come when you do not discern your placement within the Body of Christ. The good news is that Jesus the Intercessor is our example and standard. He represents the authority and benefits that come with being an intercessor. We all are participants of this grace, so when you embrace becoming an intercessor, you also open the door to friendship with God.

Paul was not attempting to be mean or discrediting in his words. He was simply concerned about the health of the people he loved. He did not want to see them weak. He did not want to see them sick; and he certainly did not want them to sleep prematurely because of their lack of discernment. He understood that misplaced gifts fall into the dangers of carrying burdens and responsibilities they may not be spiritually equipped to handle. Again, the spirit of the prophet is designed to carry things others may not be equipped to carry. This does not only apply to prophets. This is also the case for many other gifts, graces, and operations within the church.

"If the foot should say, "Because I am not a hand, I am not of the body," is it therefore not of the body? And if the ear should say, "Because I am not an eye, I am not of the body," is it therefore not of the body? If the whole body were an eye, where would be the hearing? If the whole were hearing, where would be the

smelling? But now God has set the members, each one of them, in the body just as He pleased. And if they were all one member, where would the body be? But now indeed there are many members, yet one body."
- 1 Corinthians 12:15-20 (NKJV)

A major part of the maturation process for believers is being comfortable in your grace while honoring the grace of others. Unfortunately, there are some gifts within the church today that are desired more than others, and this causes covetousness to exist amongst the saints. Paul was trying to get the church to understand that true authority and identity flows through our connection in Christ. Just not our connection to Christ, but in Christ. In other words, once you discover your fit you become a life giver to those connected to you. Not only that, but the doubts concerning your significance begin to fade, your purpose becomes more clear and your confidence increases.

We have explored many of the dynamics of both the intercessor and the prophet. Many of which I believe are significant principles you should understand in order to manifest your full prophetic potential. For some of you, more clarity has been brought concerning where you fit in the prophetic plan of God. Others of you have come to understand where the lines may have been blurred and you now have to make a decision on which side of the line you belong.

The fact of the matter is that God desires for you to find your fit. Some of you were like a square peg in a round hole because you lacked language concerning your prophetic makeup. For intercessors, your prophetic grace is driven by your prayer assignment. For prophets, many of your prayer assignments are driven by your prophetic mandate, so it is important to understand the foundation of your prophetic design.

Whether you knew it or not, your placement matters. Discerning your fit is the key to the abundance of grace in your life. As God reveals your purpose, may you embrace it and may it solidify you in your identity. Now is the greatest time for you to find your place in God's prophetic plan and to be who God called you to be.

Made in the USA
Middletown, DE
29 May 2021